Keto Mediterranean Diet Cookbook 2019

How I Lost 125 Pounds

Linda Dukly

By reading this document, the reader agrees that under no circumstances are we responsible for any losses, direct or indirect, which are incurred as a result of the use of information contained within this document, including, but not limited to, errors, omissions, or inaccuracies.

Table of contents

Introduction 8

Chapter1: Understanding the Keto diet.. 9

The history of Keto 9

The process of ketosis 9

Reaching ketosis 10

Benefits of Ketogenic diet... 12

Keto diet side effects 13

Why is keto diet suitable for most of Americans?.. 15

Chapter2: What is the Mediterranean Diet 16

The history of the Mediterranean Diet 16

Benefits of the Mediterranean Diet... 17

The Science Behind the Mediterranean Diet 18

Chapter3: Food to Eat and Food to Avoid 21

Chapter4: Tips for Ketogenic Mediterranean Diet.............................. 23

Tip#1 Try Intermittent Fasting.. 23

Tip #2 Decrease Stress 23

Tip #3 Add More Salt To Diet.. 23

Tip #4 Exercise Frequently 24

Tip #5 Batch Cooking 24

Chapter5: Breakfast 25

Spinach & Feta Omelet 25

Pesto Scrambled Eggs 27

Caprese Omelet... 28

Olive & Herb Focaccia 29

Savory Pancake 31

Mushroom Risotto 32

Frittata with Tomatoes and Cheese 33

Chapter6: Poultry 34

Tuscan Garlic Chicken 34

Garlic & Rosemary Lamb Lollipops 35

Greek Chicken 36

Lemon Chicken 38

Chicken Pesto Meatballs 40

Parmesan Chicken 41

Sun-Dried Tomato Chicken 42

Garlic Parmesan Chicken Wings 43

Chapter7: Snacks 44

Antipasto Salad 44

Pesto Pull-Apart Bread 45

Baked Halloumi Fries 47

Stuffed Peppers 48

Bruschetta Stuffed Avocado 49

Cucumber Soup 50

Zucchini Fritters 51

Eggplant Parmesan 52

Chapter8: Vegetarian 54

Roasted Asparagus 54

Cauliflower Parmesan Soup 55

Tomato Mozzarella Salad 57

Dumplings 58

Roasted Brussels Sprouts 60

Cauliflower Mash 61

Braised Fennel with Lemon 62

Roasted Broccoli 63

Chapter 9: Pork **64**

Meatloaf 64

Pork Tenderloin 66

Dijon Pork Chops 67

Pork Cutlets 68

Pork Carnitas 69

Pork Spare Ribs 71

Jamaican Jerk Pork Roast 72

Pulled Pork 73

Chapter 10: Beef **74**

Sun-Dried Tomato Cheesy Meatballs 74

Rib-eye Steak with Gremolata 76

Beef Stir-Fry 77

Sesame Beef 78

Mediterranean Burgers 80

Sirloin Beef Roast 81

Beef & Broccoli 82

Eggplant Ground Beef Skillet 83

Chapter 11: Seafood & Fish **84**

Swordfish 84

Garlic Shrimp Zoodles 85

Salmon with Asparagus 86

Tuna Salad...87

Seared Scallops..88

Grilled Sardines 89

Salmon Cakes..90

Mussels 92

Chapter12: Desserts **93**

Crème Anglaise 93

Chocolate Mousse..94

Mint Chocolate Chip Ice Cream...95

Chocolate Avocado Pudding 96

Vanilla Frozen Yogurt...97

Chia Berry Yogurt Parfaits 98

Lemon Meringue Cookies 99

Strawberry Cheesecake Jars 100

Conclusion..**101**

Introduction

Over the past ten years, numerous health researchers have forces doctors and dieticians to change the notion of a healthy diet. As a result, new discoveries have been made that tells more about the true causes and mechanisms of harmful ailments like cancer, diabetes and coronary diseases and for this reason, the previous concept for healthy food has been disregard. Recent research has provided evidence of the benefits of healthy fats in the diet, and this led to the development of the Ketogenic diet. The ketogenic diet is a low-carb and high-fat diet that has become a cornerstone for quick loss of weight. As a result, the Ketogenic diet is associated with improved blood pressure, blood glucose and insulin levels.

There is another diet that has become a widely accepted nutritional regime, Mediterranean diet. Mediterranean diet is known for prevention of coronary diseases and longevity of life. When the concept for high-fat Ketogenic diet is combined with nutrient density and lifestyle factors of traditional Mediterranean diet, a new diet comes into the light - Ketogenic Mediterranean diet.

Ketogenic Mediterranean diet features food that contains 7 to 10 percent carbohydrates, 55 to 65 percent fats, 25 to 30 percent proteins, and 5 to 10 percent alcohol. It is very easy to merge the Mediterranean diet with the Ketogenic diet. Both diets promote eating whole-foods including fresh non-starchy vegetables and fruits, proteins from fish along with eggs, cheese, poultry and meat, high amounts of healthy oils, moderate intake of red wine, and avoiding foods that are processed or contain sugars, chemicals or additives. The only difference in this diet is slight emphasize of different sources of fats and allowing red wine.

In the following chapters of this eBook, you will find more information about what Ketogenic diet and the Mediterranean diet is and how their pair is excellent for you.

Chapter 1: Understanding the Keto diet

The history of Keto

The ketogenic diet, the latest trend in the healthiest diets, is not something new. In medicine, a high fat Ketogenic diet has been in use to treat epilepsy for almost 100 years. Ketogenic diet dates back to 1920s when doctors were trying hard to find a solution for epilepsy. Though some remedies were already a part of treatment like fasting and other dietary regimens, the doctors were looking for something more permanent, and they found that a low-carb and high-fat diet was most effective to control the seizures in their epileptic patients. Hence, the doctors created a high-fat diet which they named as Ketogenic diet. At that time, the Ketogenic diet was simply a nutritious meal plan that forces the body to use fat for energy, instead of carbohydrates. The epileptic patient used to have meals that contain 5 to 10% carbs, 15 to 30 percent protein and 60 to 75 percent fats. This meal would send the body into a state called ketosis where the body breaks the stored fat into ketones and then use them for energy. The ketogenic diet was a successful treatment and widely used for the treatment of epilepsy in children.   With the introduction of the antiepileptic drug, the use of Ketogenic diet declines significantly, however, the interest of scientist and dieticians in the Ketogenic diet exploded over the past 15 years for its amazing health benefits.

The process of ketosis

The goal of the Ketogenic diet is to send the body into ketosis. You must have heard about this word a lot and even would have read about it above, but do you know what ketosis actually is?

Ketosis is derived from the word "ketones" that are small molecules in the body used as fuel. Ketones are produced from the fats or when the blood sugar level is low. In other words, when you eat less carb or more fats and a moderate amount of protein, ketones are produced.

Our body relies on glucose, the breakdown of carbs, and in their absence or limited reserves of carbs, the body soon starts to run out of glucose. When this happens, the body turns to fats and for this, the insulin level in blood drops and the hormone that burn fats increases dramatically. The body can then turn to fats and begin using them for energy, but it cannot directly fuel on fats, the fats need to be breakdown into simpler molecules. Therefore, the fat stored in the liver breaks down into ketones and then enter into the bloodstream so that it can be used as a fuel by the cell, just like glucose.

There are two ways to enter into ketosis: following a Ketogenic diet or fasting. Usually, when the body produces over 0.5mM ketones, it is said to be in ketosis.

Reaching ketosis

Getting into ketosis is easier said than done, but not hard. Moreover, it is not something like the body is either in ketosis or not. Instead, the body can be in different degrees of ketosis, but first, you need to make your body adapt to burn fats for fuel. A basic rule to reach ketosis is strictly following the Ketogenic diet. There are other ways to achieve and increase ketosis further.

- Cutting the carbs: Just like mentioned before, you need to follow Ketogenic diet to T, and this means, eating meals that are very low in carbs. Therefore, you need to make sure that your carb intake for Ketogenic meal is around 30 grams per day. This amount of carbs is enough to force your body to deplete glycogen reserves quickly and will get you into ketosis within 2 to 3 days. You don't have to start with cutting out carbs immediately; you can limit the carbs gradually. However, if you want your body to achieve ketosis fast, then you have to reduce your carbs intake drastically.

- Increase high-quality fats: Fats make up a large part of Ketogenic meal. Make sure that your fat intake for a day is between 70 to 80 percent of total calories. This will help the transition of your body to fats quickly as a primary source of fuel. Along with this, you can consume healthy fats as well. Some great options for healthy fats are coconut oil, extra-virgin olive oil, avocado oil, macadamia nut oil, MCT oil and butter like nut butter or coconut butter. You can also eat fatty meats, nuts, and avocado.

- Maintain protein intake: Having the right proportion of protein in Ketogenic meal will help you achieve the best results. You need to eat enough protein that keeps you satisfy and helps prevent the breakdown of muscles. Make sure; you are consuming at least 0.8 g of protein per pound of your lean body mass. Further, eat high-quality protein like pasture-raised chicken and grass-fed beef.

- Do fasting: Fasting have a number of health benefits like weight loss, improved mental health and controlling blood sugar and blood pressure levels. Fasting in combination with Ketogenic can-do wonders. To achieve ketosis, you can either go for fat fasting or intermittent fasting. Eating a low-calorie food, around 1000 calories, in which 80 to 90 percent portion is fats, this is fat fasting. Intermittent fasting involves having Ketogenic food with regular breaks between 10 to 12 hours.

- Do more exercise: Ramping up your physical activity can help you get into ketosis. When you exercise, the glycogen reserves in the body depletes. So, when you do more exercise and have a low-carb food with glycogen reserves that are low, the body will turn to burn fat for energy. Therefore, doing some workout and then gradually increasing its intensity will help you induce and speed up the ketosis.

Benefits of Ketogenic diet

Though most of the people go for Ketogenic diet for weight loss, there are many other amazing benefits you can get with Ketogenic diet.

- Enhanced memory
- Cognition clarity
- Control of seizure
- Fewer migraine attacks
- Fighting with tumor and cancer (astrocytomas, prostate and gastric)
- Treat Alzheimer, Autism, Parkinson's disease
- Preventing coronary, neurologic and metabolic diseases
- Controlling blood pressure
- Improve cholesterol level
- Lower triglyceride levels
- Decrease inflammation and pain
- Improve acne, eczema, and arthritis
- Improve sleep
- Stabilize insulin levels
- Maintain uric acid levels and prevent gout
- Curb diabetes
- Treat abdominal obesity

- Keep gallbladder and intestines healthy
- Reduce the risk of gallstones
- Decrease heartburns
- Improve digestion
- Reduce gas and bloating
- Increase fertility
- Stabilize hormones, especially in women
- Promote muscle gain and improve endurance

Keto diet side effects

There are many awesome benefits you can get by adopting a low-carb Ketogenic diet like treating obesity, boost mental and physical performance and much more. However, there are some common side effects that you should be aware of and how to avoid them to make the best of Ketogenic diet.

Side effect #1: Hypoglycemia

Hypoglycemia or lowering of blood sugar level happens because your body doesn't know how to burn fats and is figuring out a way to rely on fats for energy. Due to hypoglycemia, you may feel intense hunger, dizziness, depression, irritability, lack of energy. To address this issue, you need to eat mineral rich food every 3 to 4 hours to keep you satiated. Keep your body hydrated by drinking plenty of mineral-rich drinks like broths, instead of water. Make use of exogenous ketone to train your body to use ketones as fuel. This side effect should subside within 2 to 3 weeks of beginning Ketogenic diet.

Side effect #2: Electrolyte or mineral deficiencies

On a Ketogenic diet, your body may go deficient of minerals and dehydrate due to excess excretion of minerals and toxins that pulls more water which is also excreted through the urine. The most obvious symptom is increased urination and constipation. This is a positive sign that your body is successfully adapting to ketosis. To remove this deficiency and keep hydrated, regularly take additional fluids and electrolytes. Use high-quality salt generously in your food, consume mineral-rich foods and use a magnesium supplement.

Side effect #3: Keto flu

The most well-known effect of Ketogenic diet is Keto flu. Just like its name, during Keto flu, you will feel one of the following flu-like symptoms like a headache, runny nose, fatigue, drowsiness, dizziness, nausea, muscles soreness, and insomnia. To remedy Keto flu, drink more water stirred with a little salt, take food that is rich in sodium, potassium, and magnesium, eat more fat, do some light exercise regularly, meditate and sleep more.

Side effect #4: Sugar cravings

Experiencing intense food cravings is common to have during the beginning stage of the Ketogenic diet. These cravings are for high-sugar food and fighting these cravings require great will power. You can quickly fix your food craving with having an electrolyte, going for a walk, eating protein or consuming mineral rich Ketogenic snacks like pickles.

Side effect #5: Drop in strength and physical performance

During the transition to a new fuel source that it has not had to use before, the body takes time to learn to utilize fats as fuel for energy. Therefore, during this time, you will feel reduce strength and physical energy. To boost your strength, you need to eat mineral rich food every 3 to 5 hours, eat more protein, keeping yourself hydrated and maintaining a light exercise routine.

Why is keto diet suitable for most of Americans?

Research proves that the Ketogenic diet does a better job in controlling neurologic and metabolic syndromes than a standard American diet, even with exercise. These syndromes are main causes for the majority of the ailments like abnormal cholesterol levels, high blood sugar level and high blood pressure, and the common most health condition - obesity.

Medically, a Ketogenic diet is a powerful tool to treat epilepsy, and it is an interesting alternative to accelerate weight loss, which is the main reason for Ketogenic diet fame. Other incredible health benefits of Ketogenic diet make it a versatile diet so that anyone can adopt Ketogenic diet into their lifestyle. A study was carried out where two groups of people were monitor, one following Ketogenic diet and the other one undertook a standard American diet, both doing 30 minutes of exercise for daily in 10 weeks period. By the end of this study, the Ketogenic diet group showed the best results and outperformed in weight loss and overall health variables. This shows that a hearty Ketogenic diet containing fresh vegetables, fruits, whole foods, healthy oils and moderate amounts of meat, poultry, and seafood tend to be more effective than other diets.

Chapter2: What is the Mediterranean Diet

The history of the Mediterranean Diet

Mediterranean Diet offers balanced food that is a combination of taste and health. Its goal is to preserve the health of individuals by satisfying the body with gastronomic foods that help the body to perform the vital function effectively. The name of this healthy diet is a combination of two words – 'Mediterranean' and 'Diet.' The Mediterranean is the name of the sea connecting Asia, Europe, and Africa and it is in the countries surrounding this sea, including Greece, Southern Italy, Crete, Spain, France, Israel, Turkey, and Morocco, where Mediterranean diet originated. The Mediterranean diet is base on the eating patterns of these Mediterranean regions and their traditional dishes. The Mediterranean regions have been a crossroad for many civilizations, cultures and religious practices that have influences traditional dishes. The Mediterranean regions are abundant with olives, rich seasonal fruits, fresh greens, Mediterranean herbs, wheat, grain, lots of seafood, other natural whole foods and local products and these components became the essential part of the diet for the people living in the Mediterranean areas. The most iconic Mediterranean dishes are tomato pesto, couscous made with a variety of local seafood, vegetables, legume, and salads like Pantescan salad, eggplant caponata and more.

Though Mediterranean diet has been in practice for over 5000 years, it was actually developed in the 1960s and did not gain much attention until 1975 when this diet was studied and experimented for heart diseases. Mediterranean diet is high in fat and cholesterol that are the major causes for heart disease, but research conducted in 1975 showed that the inhabitants of Mediterranean regions had significantly lower risks of developing heart disease and higher average life expectancy than Americans, despite having limited access to healthcare. By 1990s, the diet gains more popularity among the public due to being rich in fish, olive oil and natural foods.

Benefits of the Mediterranean Diet

A Mediterranean diet offers a healthy food option along with a way of healthy living routine by respecting the environment, cultures, and religions. The Mediterranean herbs and plants contain medicinal properties and widely used for medical treatment, thus saving people's lives. This diet has been examine for its health outcomes for more than 50 years, and the research showed that the Mediterranean lowers the risk of developing cardiovascular diseases. At the forefront, new researches have led to the growing of more incredible health benefits that have risen this diet to curb health issues. Mediterranean diet is now linked with an array of health benefits including:

- Longer life span,
- Weight loss,
- Appetite Reduction,
- Improved brain function,
- Controlling rheumatoid arthritis,
- Enhance vision,
- Lower risks of developing cancers,
- Treatment for heart disease, Alzheimer's disease, and diabetes,
- Lower levels of blood pressure and LDL cholesterol.

The Science Behind the Mediterranean Diet

Mediterranean diet is a heart-healthy diet. Research has shown that the Mediterranean diet is perfect for treating chronic diseases like heart stroke and high blood pressure. It lowers the level of bad cholesterol (low-density lipoprotein (LDL)) that builds deposits in your arteries. In fact, the Mediterranean diet is associated with preventing cancer, Parkinson's and Alzheimer's diseases. For women, the Mediterranean diet reduces the risk of developing breast cancer. So how does it work?

- **Eating plan**

Mediterranean diet is not a magic bullet, and neither is it about eating one particular food. It is about eating simple and nutrient-dense foods. It is about making the most of the available food and savoring their flavors. These key characteristics make the Mediterranean diet incredibly easy to adapt in daily lifestyle. Some additional points will help your body to achieve the best from the Mediterranean diet.

Emphasize on eating healthy fats. Olive oil is generally recommended as the primary source of fats in the Mediterranean diet, discouraging the use of saturated fats and hydrogenated fats as they contribute to heart diseases. Make use of virgin or extra-virgin olive oil because they are the least processed forms of olive oil and contains the highest level of antioxidant that is beneficial for health. For a change in taste, you can replace olive oil with other high-fat and oils such as avocado oil, coconut oil, and butter. Moreover, consume other foods that contain healthy fats such as avocados, nuts, seeds, walnuts and fish and seafood that are high in omega-3 fatty acids such as tuna, salmon, sardine, trout, and mackerel.

Eat protein in the right amount. In the Mediterranean diet, the preferred protein source is fish and seafood, but it doesn't have to be the only source of animal protein. Add variation by consuming proteins from eggs, dairy products, poultry like chicken, lamb, turkey, pork. You can also have red meat in moderate amount. Drink more water. Choose water as your main beverage and drink it plentifully. You can allow yourself a joy of wine (moderate amount), about 1 to 2 glasses daily for men and one glass a day for women.

- Healthy Lifestyle

Along with food, lifestyle factor plays an important role in helping the Mediterranean diet to make a difference in your health. These factors can be loving your community, stress management, maintaining physical activity, sleep and hygiene habits. Health lifestyle habits create a positive impact on health such as lowering the risk of heart diseases and body mass index, reduce stress and last but not the least, it provides a great sense of life satisfaction. To achieve a healthy lifestyle, you need to

Prioritize your sleep hygiene. Sleep is often overlooked in other diets, but in a Mediterranean diet, you cannot compromise on your sleep. To improve the quality of your sleep, you can try to sleep in a dark and cool place. You need to complete your sleep cycle and make sure you are not waking up in the middle of deep sleep.

D0 physical activity regularly. Physical activity is not just a weight loss tool; it is a wellness tool as well. Start with moderate physical activity and when you get successful in maintaining it, switch to vigorous physical activity.

Love life. One of the aspects of the Mediterranean lifestyle is loving your family, spending fun time with friends and relatives and appreciating your community.

These little acts of love and kindness will fill your heart with merriment and relax your mind.

Chapter3: Food to Eat and Food to Avoid

Despite an emphasis on legumes, wheat, grains, and certain vegetables, the Mediterranean diet is compatible with a low-carb and high-fat eating lifestyle. Here is the list of items you can eat and avoid in Mediterranean Ketogenic Diet.

What to Eat Abundantly:

1- Fish and all kind of seafood
2- Low-carb vegetables such as the one that grows above the ground such as greens, broccoli, cauliflower, avocado, lettuce, herbs, a moderate amount of nightshade vegetables and sweet peppers
3- Low-carb fruits such berries
4- Sweeteners such as monk fruit sweetener and Erythritol
5- Healthy oils such as olive oil
6- Nuts and seeds such as almonds, walnuts, hazelnuts, pistachio, macadamia nuts, peanuts, sesame seeds.
7- Wine – red wine

What to Eat Moderately:

1- Avocado oil and coconut oil
2- Lean meat and poultry
3- High-fat cheeses
4- Greek Yogurt and cream
5- Eggs

What Not to Eat:

1- Wheat

2- Beans

3- Legumes, pulses, and millet

4- Rice, grains, cereals

5- Pasta and bread

6- Starchy vegetables like potatoes, corn, and peas.

7- All foods containing sugar and flour like bread and cakes.

Chapter4: Tips for Ketogenic Mediterranean Diet

Tip#1 Try Intermittent Fasting

When you are going for Ketogenic Mediterranean diet, you have to be in ketosis as soon as possible. The fastest and most effective way to get into ketosis is intermittent fasting. Your body needs first to burn all its glucose, and only then, it will switch to fats for fuel – the whole point of ketosis. When you will not consume any food or drink anything for a few hours, the glucose reserve will start depleting and then will start burning fats for energy. If you are a beginner to Ketogenic Mediterranean diet, skip breakfast for no more than 3 to 5 days to enter ketosis faster.

Tip #2 Decrease Stress

One of the goals of Ketogenic Mediterranean diet is to enjoy your food and savor its taste, and for that, you need to be stress-free and relax. Elevated stress hormones will elevate sugar levels in the blood, and this will prevent your body from burning fat. Therefore, you need to keep your stress to a minimum level if you want to begin with Ketogenic Mediterranean diet plan and keep yourself devoted to it. You can reduce your stress by taking proper sleep, meditating or doing yoga, exercising regularly and spending the time to do something you enjoy.

Tip #3 Add More Salt To Diet

Both Mediterranean and Ketogenic diet is higher in salt and this help in avoiding electrolyte/mineral imbalance. When the body adopts are high-fat and low-carb diet, it excretes more salt and water due to the absence of carbohydrates for energy. This will make you feel low in strength and dehydrated and will disturb the process of ketosis in your body. To avoid this, add an extra 3 g to 5 g salt in the form of sprinkling salt on your food, eating salted nuts, consuming low carb foods that contain natural sodium or drinking bone broth.

Tip #4 Exercise Frequently

Regular exercise will uplift your mood along with boosting your ketones level. Be sure to maintain your exercise, begin with light exercise and then move on to a high-intensity workout. When you are working out, the water in the body will excrete in the form of urine and sweat so drink more after an intense workout or on hot summer days.

Tip #5 Batch Cooking

Be it any diet; you don't have to cook every meal each day. You can opt an alternative way for healthy and tasty food through batch cooking. Just like batch cooking sounds, you will cook a big batch of meal that you can freeze and reheat whenever you feel hungry. Yes, batch cooking does need a lot of work, but it is one time and need the same amount of time that just one meal takes for cooking, irrespective to cooking three times a day. Further, it reduces food waste and will help you save serious money. In the next chapter, you will find Ketogenic version of your favorite foods that are rich in Mediterranean colors, flavors, and taste.

Chapter5: Breakfast

Spinach & Feta Omelet

Servings: 1
Preparation time: 5 minutes; Active cooking time: 5 minutes; Total time: 10 minutes

Nutrition Value:
Calories: 659 Cal, Carbs: 9.7 g, Fat: 55.5 g, Protein: 30.9 g, Fiber: 2.8 g.

Ingredients:
- 3 cups spinach, fresh
- 1 cup white mushrooms, sliced
- ½ teaspoon minced garlic
- 1 teaspoon salt
- ½ teaspoon cracked black pepper
- 2 tablespoons olive oil
- 1/3 cup feta cheese, crumbled
- 3 eggs, pasture-raised

Method:
1. Place a large skillet pan over medium-high heat, add 1 tablespoon olive oil and garlic, season with ½ teaspoon salt and cook for 1 minute or until fragrant.
2. Add mushrooms and cook for 5 minutes or until nicely golden brown.
3. Then add spinach and cook for 1 to 2 minutes or until spinach leaves wilt.
4. Spoon this mixture into a bowl, discarding excess liquid from the pan, returning pan to the stove.
5. Add eggs and mix until well combined and season with remaining salt and black pepper.
6. Add 1 tablespoon oil into the pan, add egg mixture and bring the egg mixture to the center from pan from the sides with a spatula.
7. Reduce heat to lower level and cook the omelet for 1 minute or more until soft and fluffy.

8. Spread spinach-mushroom mixture evenly on top of the omelet, scatter with cheese and then fold in half.
9. Cook omelet for 1 minute or until topping is warmed through and then slide onto serving plate.
10. Serve immediately.

Pesto Scrambled Eggs

Servings: 1

Preparation time: 5 minutes; Active cooking time: 5 minutes; Total time: 10 minutes

Nutrition Value:

Calories: 467 Cal, Carbs: 3.3 g, Fat: 41.5 g, Protein: 20.4 g, Fiber: 0.7 g.

Ingredients:
- 3 eggs, pasture-raised
- ½ teaspoon salt
- ½ teaspoon cracked black pepper
- 1 tablespoon unsalted butter
- 1 tablespoon olive oil
- 1 tablespoon basil pesto, fresh
- 2 tablespoons soured cream, full-fat

Method:
1. Crack eggs in a bowl, season with salt and black pepper and blend well with a whisker.
2. Place a medium skillet pan over low heat, pour in egg mixture, add butter and oil and stir well with a whisker.
3. Then whisk in pesto and cook for 1 to 2 minutes or until creamy scrambled eggs come together.
4. Remove pan from heat, stir in sour cream until well mixed and spoon scrambled eggs into serving plate.
5. Serve straightaway.

Caprese Omelet

Servings: 1
Preparation time: 5 minutes; Active cooking time: 5 minutes; Total time: 10 minutes

Nutrition Value:
Calories: 533 Cal, Carbs: 4.9 g, Fat: 43.2 g, Protein: 30.8 g, Fiber: 1.1 g.

Ingredients:
- 1/3 cup cherry tomatoes, halved
- 6 basil leaves, chopped
- 1/2 teaspoon sea salt
- 1/4 teaspoon cracked black pepper
- 1 tablespoon basil pesto, fresh
- 1 tablespoon olive oil and more for drizzling
- 3 eggs, pasture-raised
- 2 slices of fresh mozzarella cheese, full-fat
- 1 tablespoon grated Parmesan cheese, full-fat

Method:
1. Crack the eggs in a bowl and whisk until blended.
2. Place a small skillet pan over low heat, add oil and when hot, pour in eggs and bring the egg mixture to the center from pan from the sides with a spatula.
3. Then top one half of egg with half of the tomatoes, basil leaves, and cheeses and fold the other half of Caprese to cover this topping.
4. Cook omelet for 1 minute or until Caprese is set and then slide onto serving plate.
5. Drizzle Caprese with basil pesto and olive oil, top with remaining tomatoes and serve straightaway.

Olive & Herb Focaccia

Servings: 4

Preparation time: 10 minutes; Active cooking time: 15 minutes; Total time: 25 minutes

Nutrition Value:

Calories: 144 Cal, Carbs: 4.8 g, Fat: 10.9 g, Protein: 6.6 g, Fiber: 3 g.

Ingredients:

- 1/4 cup sliced kalamata olives, fresh
- 1/3 cup and 1 tablespoon coconut flour
- 2 1/2 tablespoons psyllium husks
- 1 teaspoon baking powder
- 1/2 teaspoon salt
- 1 tablespoon minced fresh rosemary
- 1 tablespoon minced fresh sage
- 2 tablespoons olive oil
- 4 eggs, pasture-raised
- 2 tablespoons Greek yogurt

Method:

1. Set oven to 375 degrees F and let preheat.
2. In the meantime, crack eggs in a bowl, add yogurt and whisk until combined.
3. Place flour in another bowl, add psyllium husks, baking powder, and salt and stir until just mixed.
4. Add egg mixture and stir well until soft dough comes together.
5. Take a baking sheet, line with parchment paper, place dough on it and shape into a ½-inch thick rectangle.
6. Place a small saucepan over low heat, add salt, minced rosemary, and sage, 1 tablespoon olive oil and cook for 1 to 2 minutes or until fragrant.
7. Spoon this mixture over dough, then scatter with olive and drizzle with remaining oil and place baking tray into the heated oven.
8. Bake Focaccia for 15 minutes or until top is nicely golden brown and cooked through.

9. When done, slice to serve.

Savory Pancake

Servings: 1
Preparation time: 5 minutes; Active cooking time: 10 minutes; Total time: 15 minutes

Nutrition Value:
Calories: 294 Cal, Carbs: 3.8 g, Fat: 21.7 g, Protein: 19 g, Fiber: 1.5 g.

Ingredients:
- 2 tablespoons coconut flour
- 2 tablespoons chopped chives
- ½ teaspoon salt
- ¼ teaspoon cracked black pepper
- 1/4 teaspoon apple cider vinegar
- 1 tablespoon olive oil
- 3 eggs, pasture-raised
- 1/2 cup grated Parmesan cheese, full-fat

Method:
1. Separate egg yolks and egg whites in two bowls.
2. Into egg whites, add vinegar and beat using a stand mixer until stiff peaks forms.
3. Then fold in egg yolks, cheese, flour, chives, salt and black pepper with a whisker.
4. Place a small skillet pan over medium heat, add oil and when hot, pour in pancake mixture.
5. Cook for 3 minutes or until bottom sets and bubbles appear on top.
6. Turn on broiler, place pan containing pancake into the broiler and cook for 3 to 5 minutes or until top is nicely golden brown.
7. When done, slide pancake to a serving plate and serve.

Mushroom Risotto

Servings: 2
Preparation time: 20 minutes; **Active cooking time:** 20 minutes; **Total time:** 40 minutes

Nutrition Value:
Calories: 287 Cal, Carbs: 11.3 g, Fat: 24.4 g, Protein: 8 g, Fiber: 3.4 g.

Ingredients:
- 6 cups riced cauliflower, fresh
- ½ cup dried porcini mushrooms, organic
- 4 cups fresh wild mushrooms, chopped
- ¼ cup chopped fresh parsley
- 1 small white onion, peeled and sliced
- 1 teaspoon minced garlic
- 1 tablespoon lemon juice
- ¼ cup and 2 tablespoons olive oil
- ½ cup heavy whipping cream, full-fat
- ⅔ cup grated parmesan cheese, full-fat
- ¾ cup chicken broth, pasture-raised

Method:
1. Pour chicken broth in a bowl, add porcini mushrooms and let soak for 15 minutes.
2. Then place a large skillet pan over medium-high heat, add ½ cup oil and when hot, add onion and garlic.
3. Cook for 5 to 8 minutes or until nicely golden brown, then wild mushrooms and cauliflower rice and stir well.
4. Add soaked porcini mushrooms along with their liquid, season with salt, stir in cream and cook risotto for 8 to 10 minutes or until cauliflower is tender.
5. Remove pan from heat, drizzle remaining olive oil and lemon juice over risotto, sprinkle with cheese and stir until combined.
6. Serve straightaway.

Frittata with Tomatoes and Cheese

Servings: 2
Preparation time: 10 minutes; Active cooking time: 15 minutes; Total time: 25 minutes

Nutrition Value:
Calories: 435 Cal, Carbs: 6.2 g, Fat: 32.6 g, Protein: 26.7 g, Fiber: 1.2 g.

Ingredients:
- 1/2 of medium white onion, peeled and sliced
- 2/3 cup cherry tomatoes, halved
- 2 tablespoons chopped basil, fresh
- ½ teaspoon salt
- ½ teaspoon cracked black pepper
- 1 tablespoon olive oil
- 6 eggs, pasture-raised
- 2/3 cup full-fat feta cheese, crumbled

Method:
1. Set oven to 400 degrees F and let preheat.
2. In the meantime, place a medium skillet pan over medium heat and when hot, add oil and onion and cook for 3 to 5 minutes or until nicely golden brown.
3. While onions are cooking, crack eggs in a bowl, add basil, season with salt and black pepper and whisk until blended.
4. Pour this mixture into onion mixture and cook for 1 to 2 minutes or until edges start turning opaque.
5. Then top frittata with tomatoes and cheese and transfer pan into the oven.
6. Cook for 5 to 7 minutes or until frittata is cook through and the top is nicely golden brown.
7. Serve straightaway.

Chapter6: Poultry

Tuscan Garlic Chicken

Servings: 4

Preparation time: 5 minutes; Active cooking time: 10 minutes; Total time: 15 minutes

Nutrition Value:

Calories: 487.7 Cal, Carbs: 7.3 g, Fat: 35.8 g, Protein: 33.8 g, Fiber: 1.2 g.

Ingredients:

- 1½ pounds skinless pasture-raised chicken breasts, thinly sliced
- 1 cup fresh spinach, chopped
- ½ cup sun-dried tomatoes
- 1 teaspoon garlic powder
- 1 teaspoon Italian seasoning
- 2 tablespoons olive oil
- ½ cup parmesan cheese, full-fat
- 1 cup heavy cream, full-fat
- ½ cup chicken broth, pasture-raised

Method:

1. Place a large skillet over high heat, add oil and when hot, add chicken breast pieces.
2. Cook for 3 to 5 minutes or until nicely golden brown on each side and then transfer chicken pieces to a plate.
3. Return pan over medium-high heat, add remaining ingredients except for spinach and tomatoes and whisk well.
4. Cook for 1 to 2 minutes or until mixture starts to thicken, then add spinach and tomatoes and simmer for 3 minutes or until spinach leaves wilt.
5. Return chicken to pan and stir well.
6. Serve when ready.

Garlic & Rosemary Lamb Lollipops

Servings: 2

Preparation time: 10 minutes; Active cooking time: 10 minutes; Total time: 20 minutes

Nutrition Value:

Calories: 171.5 Cal, Carbs: 0.4 g, Fat: 7.8 g, Protein: 23.2 g, Fiber: 0.1 g.

Ingredients:
- 8 lamb lollipops, pastured
- 2 tablespoons rosemary leaves
- 1 teaspoon minced garlic
- 1 teaspoon salt
- ¾ teaspoon cracked black pepper
- 3 tablespoons olive oil

Method:
1. Season lamb with salt and black pepper on each side and then sprinkle with 1 tablespoon rosemary leaves.
2. Place a large skillet pan over medium-high heat, add oil and when hot, add remaining rosemary leaves and garlic and then lamb lollipops.
3. Cook lamb lollipops for 5 minutes per side until seared.
4. Serve immediately.

Greek Chicken

Servings: 4

Preparation time: 1 hour and 10 minutes; Active cooking time: 16 minutes; Total time: 1 hour and 26 minutes

Nutrition Value:
Calories: 261 Cal, Carbs: 1.8 g, Fat: 19 g, Protein: 21 g, Fiber: 1.5 g.

Ingredients:
- 4 skinless chicken breasts, pasture-raised
- 1 cup chopped cherry tomatoes
- 1/3 cup sliced Kalamata olives
- 2 teaspoons minced garlic
- 3 tablespoons chopped oregano, fresh
- 1 teaspoon salt
- ¾ teaspoon cracked black pepper
- 1/2 cup and 2 tablespoons olive oil
- 1/2 cup lemon juice
- 1/2 cup crumbled Feta cheese, full-fat

Method:
1. Score top of each chicken breast in crisscross and place in a re-sealable plastic bag.
2. Whisk together garlic, oregano, lemon juice, and ½ cup olive oil until combined, reserve ¼ cup of this mixture and pour remaining mixture into a plastic bag containing chicken pieces.
3. Seal the bag, turn it upside until chicken pieces are well coated and let marinate in the refrigerator for 1 hour.
4. When ready to cook, take out the chicken from the refrigerator and let rest at room temperature.
5. In the meantime, place reserved marinade in a bowl, add tomatoes, olives, and cheese and toss until well coated.
6. Place a large skillet pan over medium-high heat, add 1 tablespoon oil and when hot, add marinated chicken in a single layer, scored side down.

7. Cook for 4 minutes per side or until chicken is no longer pink, then season with salt and black and transfer to a plate.
8. Add remaining oil to the pan and cook remaining chicken in the same manner.
9. Top chicken with tomato-olives-feta topping and serve.

Lemon Chicken

Servings: 4

Preparation time: 10 minutes; **Active cooking time:** 15 minutes; **Total time:** 25 minutes

Nutrition Value:

Calories: 282 Cal, Carbs: 5 g, Fat: 18 g, Protein: 26 g, Fiber: 1 g.

Ingredients:

- 1-pound skinless pasture-raised chicken breast, cut into 4 slices
- 1 cup cherry tomatoes
- 1/2 cup white onions, peeled and cut into 1/4-inch slices
- 1 teaspoon minced garlic
- 1/2 teaspoon onion powder
- 1/2 teaspoon garlic powder
- 1 teaspoon salt
- 1/4 teaspoon cracked black pepper, freshly ground
- 1/2 teaspoon paprika
- 2 sprigs of thyme
- 3 sprigs of rosemary
- 1 1/2 teaspoons ground cumin
- 1/2 teaspoon ground coriander
- 1/4 cup olive oil
- 3 tablespoons lemon juice

Method:

1. Stir together onion powder, garlic powder, salt, black pepper, paprika, cumin and coriander in a bowl.
2. Sprinkle ½ teaspoon of this spice mix on each side of the chicken piece.
3. Place a large skillet pan over medium-high heat, add oil and when hot, add onion and garlic.
4. Cook for 2 minutes, move to the side and then add tomatoes to the pan.
5. Cook tomatoes for 3 minutes and then transfer onion and tomatoes to a bowl.

6. Add thyme and rosemary sprigs to skillet pan, then add seasoned chicken to the pan and cook for 4 to 5 minutes per side or until chicken is nicely browned.
7. Then remove the pan from heat, drizzle with lemon juice, top with onion and tomatoes and serve.

Chicken Pesto Meatballs

Servings: 20
Preparation time: 10 minutes; **Active cooking time:** 20 minutes; **Total time:** 30 minutes

Nutrition Value:
Calories: 424 Cal, Carbs: 6.2 g, Fat: 32.9 g, Protein: 27.3 g, Fiber: 1.9 g.

Ingredients:
- 1-pound ground chicken, pasture-raised
- 1 small red onion, peeled and chopped
- 1/2 cup almond flour
- 1/2 teaspoon sea salt
- 1/2 cup basil pesto, divided
- 1 egg, pasture-raised

Method:
1. Set oven to 375 degrees F and let preheat.
2. In the meantime, place chicken in a bowl, add onion, flour, salt, ¼ cup pesto, and egg and stir until well combined.
3. Shape this mixture into 16 meatballs and place onto a baking sheet, greased with olive oil.
4. Place the baking sheet into the heated oven and bake for 20 minutes or until nicely golden brown and cooked through.
5. When done, transfer meatballs to a serving plate, top with remaining pesto and serve.

Parmesan Chicken

Servings: 6

Preparation time: 10 minutes; Active cooking time: 30 minutes; Total time: 40 minutes

Nutrition Value:

Calories: 454 Cal, Carbs: 9.1 g, Fat: 24.8 g, Protein: 49.4 g, Fiber: 7.6 g.

Ingredients:
- 6 skinless chicken breasts, pasture-raised
- 1/2 teaspoon garlic powder
- 1/2 teaspoon sea salt
- 1/2 teaspoon cracked black pepper
- 1/2 teaspoon dried oregano
- 1/2 cup and 1 tablespoon mayonnaise, full-fat
- 2/3 cup grated Parmesan cheese, full-fat
- 3/4 cup and 1 tablespoon coconut flakes, dried

Method:
1. Set oven to 430 degrees F and let preheat.
2. In the meantime, stir together garlic powder, garlic powder, salt, black pepper, oregano, coconut flakes and cheese in a bowl.
3. Place mayonnaise in another bowl.
4. Working on one chicken piece at a time, first season with salt, then coat with mayonnaise and cover evenly with flake mixture.
5. Place coated chicken breasts on a baking tray, lined with parchment sheet and place into the heated oven.
6. Bake for 30 minutes or until top is nicely browned and cooked through.
7. When done, slice chicken or serve straight away.

Sun-Dried Tomato Chicken

Servings: 6

Preparation time: 10 minutes; Active cooking time: 18 minutes; Total time: 28 minutes

Nutrition Value:

Calories: 553 Cal, Carbs: 7.5 g, Fat: 43.4 g, Protein: 32.2 g, Fiber: 1.4 g.

Ingredients:

- 6 skinless, boneless chicken thighs, pasture-raised
- 1 cup sun-dried tomatoes, chopped
- 2 teaspoons minced garlic
- 1 teaspoon sea salt
- 1/2 teaspoon cracked black pepper
- 1 tablespoon Italian seasoning
- 1/4 cup olive oil, from sun-dried tomato jar
- 3/4 cup grated Parmesan cheese, divided
- 1 1/2 cup heavy whipping cream, full-fat

Method:

1. Stir together salt, black pepper, and ½ cup cheese in a bowl and dredge each chicken in this mixture until well coated on all sides.
2. Place a large skillet pan over medium-high heat, add oil and when hot, add coated chicken thighs.
3. Sear chicken thighs for 5 minutes per side until nicely golden brown on all sides and then transfer to a plate, set aside until required.
4. Add tomatoes to the pan along with garlic and Italian seasoning and cook for 2 minutes or until fragrant.
5. Stir in remaining cheese and cream until combined, return chicken to pan and cook for 5 minutes.
6. Serve straightaway.

Garlic Parmesan Chicken Wings

Servings: 4

Preparation time: 10 minutes; Active cooking time: 35 minutes; Total time: 45 minutes

Nutrition Value:

Calories: 259 Cal, Carbs: 1.2 g, Fat: 20.3 g, Protein: 17.5 g, Fiber: 0.1 g.

Ingredients:

- 16 chicken wings, pasture-raised
- 2 teaspoons minced garlic
- 2 teaspoons minced parsley
- 1/4 cup olive oil
- ¼ cup unsalted butter
- 1 cup grated Parmesan cheese, full-fat
- 2 tablespoons chopped basil leaves

Method:

1. Set oven to 450 degrees F and let preheat.
2. In the meantime, place a large skillet pan over medium-high heat, add oil and when hot, add chicken wings.
3. Cook for 3 minutes per side until seared and then transfer pan to heated oven.
4. Bake chicken wings for 20 to 30 minutes or until nicely golden brown and crispy.
5. When done, return pan over medium heat, add garlic and butter and cook until butter melt completely and chicken is well coated with butter-garlic mixture.
6. Sprinkle cheese over chicken wings and remove the pan from heat.
7. Garnish with basil and serve.

Chapter7: Snacks

Antipasto Salad

Servings: 4
Preparation time: 5 minutes; Active cooking time: 0 minute; Total time: 5 minutes

Nutrition Value:
Calories: 462 Cal, Carbs: 7 g, Fat: 41 g, Protein: 14 g, Fiber: 3 g.

Ingredients:
- 4 ounces prosciutto, cut in strips
- 4 ounces pepperoni, cubed
- 1 large head romaine hearts, chopped
- 1/2 cup artichoke hearts, sliced
- ¼ cup green olives
- ¼ cup black olives
- 1/2 cup sweet peppers, roasted
- 2 tablespoons Italian dressing

Method:
1. Prepare all the ingredients and place into a bowl.
2. Add Italian dressing, toss until ingredients are well coated and serve.

Pesto Pull-Apart Bread

Servings: 12
Preparation time: 10 minutes; Active cooking time: 60 minutes; Total time: 70 minutes

Nutrition Value:
Calories: 236 Cal, Carbs: 10.4 g, Fat: 19 g, Protein: 10 g, Fiber: 6.7 g.

Ingredients:
- 1/2 cup pecans
- 1 bunch fresh basil
- 2 cups arugula
- 2 teaspoons minced garlic
- ½ teaspoon sea salt
- ½ teaspoon ground black pepper
- 2 teaspoons lemon zest
- 1/4 cup olive oil
- 1 tbsp lemon juice
- 1/2 cup grated Parmesan cheese, full-fat
- 12 sourdough baguettes dough, low-carb

Method:
1. Set oven to 325 degrees F and let preheat.
2. In the meantime, prepare pesto and for this, place pecans, basil, arugula, garlic, salt, black pepper, lemon zest, and lemon juice.
3. Pulse for smooth, then gradually blend in olive oil until combined and tip pesto into a bowl.
4. Place dough onto a clean working space, shape into 12 portions, then place 1 tablespoon prepared pesto into the center of each dough and roll into balls.
5. Take a large skillet pan, grease with olive oil and arrange the prepare dough balls in the bottom of the pan in a circular pattern.
6. Top with parmesan cheese until all dough balls are covered and then place pan into the heated oven.

7. Bake for 50 to 60 minutes or until dough balls are cook through and the top is golden brown.
8. When done, remove the pan from oven and let rest for 5 minutes.
9. Serve straightaway.

Baked Halloumi Fries

Servings: 4

Preparation time: 10 minutes; Active cooking time: 15 minutes; Total time: 25 minutes

Nutrition Value:

Calories: 292 Cal, Carbs: 4.5 g, Fat: 23 g, Protein: 15.9 g, Fiber: 2 g.

Ingredients:

- 1/3 cup coconut flour
- 1/4 teaspoon sea salt
- 1 teaspoon paprika
- 2 tablespoons olive oil
- 1 pasture-raised egg, lightly beaten
- 8.8-ounce halloumi cheese, full-fat

Method:

1. Set oven to 320 degrees F and let preheat.
2. In the meantime, cut cheese into ½-inch sticks, about 8 to 12 pieces, and pat dry with kitchen paper.
3. Stir together flour, salt, and paprika until mixed and crack the egg in another bowl.
4. Working on 1 cheese stick at a time, dredge with flour mixture, then coat with egg and cover again with flour mixture.
5. Take a baking sheet, grease with oil, place coated cheese sticks and spray with olive oil.
6. Place the baking sheet into the oven and bake for 12 to 15 minutes or until nicely golden brown.
7. Serve cheese sticks with guacamole.

Stuffed Peppers

Servings: 16
Preparation time: 5 minutes; Active cooking time: 7 minutes; Total time: 12 minutes

Nutrition Value:
Calories: 123 Cal, Carbs: 2.7 g, Fat: 9.1 g, Protein: 7.7 g, Fiber: 0.6 g.

Ingredients:
- 8 slices of prosciutto di Parma
- 16 small sweet peppers, deseeded
- 2 tablespoons minced white onion
- 1 teaspoon minced garlic
- 1 tablespoon minced parsley
- 1 tablespoon minced basil
- 1 tablespoon minced dill
- 1/2 teaspoon crushed red pepper flakes
- 1 tablespoon olive oil
- 1-pound goat cheese, full-fat
- 1/2 cup sour cream, full-fat

Method:
1. Switch on the broiler and let preheat.
2. In the meantime, stir together onion, garlic, parsley, basil, dill, red pepper flakes, and cheese and then spoon this mixture in a piping bag.
3. Remove the top from each pepper, discard the seed and then stuff with prepared cheese mixture.
4. Cut prosciutto in half lengthwise and then wrap a half slice of prosciutto on each pepper.
5. Place these peppers on a baking sheet, drizzle with oil and place the baking sheet under the broiler.
6. Cook for 5 to 7 minutes or until nicely golden brown and crispy, turning halfway through.
7. When done, let peppers cool for 5 minutes and then serve.

Bruschetta Stuffed Avocado

Servings: 2

Preparation time: 5 minutes; Active cooking time: 0 minute; Total time: 5 minutes

Nutrition Value:

Calories: 237 Cal, Carbs: 12.1 g, Fat: 21.6 g, Protein: 2.7 g, Fiber: 7.5 g.

Ingredients:

- 1 large avocado, pitted and halved
- 3.5-ounce Roma tomato, diced
- 1 tablespoon diced red onion
- 1 tablespoon chopped fresh basil
- ½ teaspoon minced garlic
- ¼ teaspoon salt
- ¼ teaspoon ground black pepper
- 1 teaspoon apple cider vinegar
- 1 tablespoon olive oil

Method:

1. Place all the ingredients in a bowl except for avocado and stir until mixed.
2. Cut avocado into half, remove its pit and then stuff with prepared bruschetta mixture.
3. Serve immediately.

Cucumber Soup

Servings: 6
Preparation time: 2 hours and 5 minutes; **Active cooking time:** 0 minutes; **Total time:** 2 hours and 5 minutes

Nutrition Value:
Calories: 266 Cal, Carbs: 9.5 g, Fat: 25.7 g, Protein: 2.4 g, Fiber: 4.9 g.

Ingredients:
- 4-pound cucumbers, chopped
- 1 medium cucumber, sliced
- 2 medium avocados
- 2 tablespoons chopped basil leaves and more for topping
- 2 large spring onions, chopped
- 1 teaspoon minced garlic
- 3/4 teaspoon sea salt
- 1/4 teaspoon cracked black pepper
- 3 tablespoons lime juice
- 1/2 cup olive oil, divided
- 2 cups chicken stock
- 1 medium cucumber, thinly sliced

Method:
1. Place chopped cucumber in a blender, add avocado, onion, garlic, basil, salt, black pepper, lime juice, olive oil, and water.
2. Pulse for 2 minutes at high speed or until smooth and creamy and then pour this mixture into a saucepan.
3. Place the saucepan into the refrigerator for 2 hours or until chilled.
4. When ready to serve, ladle soup into bowls, top with sliced cucumber and basil and serve.

Zucchini Fritters

Servings: 4

Preparation time: 5 minutes; Active cooking time: 6 minutes; Total time: 11 minutes

Nutrition Value:

Calories: 216 Cal, Carbs: 5 g, Fat: 19.8 g, Protein: 6.3 g, Fiber: 1.8 g.

Ingredients:
- 3 medium zucchini, grated
- 1/4 cup almond flour
- 1 teaspoon sea salt
- 1/4 teaspoon cracked black pepper
- 1/4 cup olive oil and more as needed
- 1 egg, pasture-raised
- 1/4 cup grated Parmesan cheese, full-fat

Method:
1. Place grated zucchini on a tea towel, wrap it and squeeze to remove excess moisture completely.
2. Then place this zucchini in a bowl, add remaining ingredients and stir until well combined.
3. Tip mixture in a shallow dish and shape mixture into 8 patties.
4. Place a large skillet pan over medium-high heat, grease with oil and when hot, add patties.
5. Cook for 2 to 3 minutes per time or until crispy and nicely golden brown.
6. Serve straightaway.

Eggplant Parmesan

Servings: 2

Preparation time: 1 hour and 10 minutes; Active cooking time: 12 minutes; Total time: 1 hour and 22 minutes

Nutrition Value:

Calories: 405 Cal, Carbs: 15.1 g, Fat: 31.2 g, Protein: 16.2 g, Fiber: 7.8 g.

Ingredients:

- 1 large eggplant
- 1/2 cup almond flour
- 1/2 cup coconut flour
- 1 teaspoon dried Italian herb
- 1 teaspoon salt, divided
- ½ teaspoon cracked black pepper
- 1/4 cup olive oil
- 1 cup grated Parmesan cheese, full-fat
- 1 egg, pasture-raised
- 1 tablespoon almond milk, unsweetened and full-fat

Method:

1. Slice eggplant widthwise into ½ inch pieces, then season with ½ teaspoon salt and let rest for 1 hour.
2. Then pat dry eggplant slices by placing an eggplant slice between two paper towel and squeeze to drain excess moisture.
3. Crack the egg in a bowl, add cream and beat with a stick blender until creamy.
4. Place Italian herbs in a shallow dish, add cheese and stir until mixed.
5. Place flours in another shallow dish and stir until mixed.
6. Working on one eggplant slice at a time, dip into egg, cover with cheese mixture and then dredge with flour mixture.
7. Place a large skillet pan over medium-high heat, add oil and when hot, add eggplant slices in a single layer.
8. Cook for 2 to 3 minutes per side or until nicely golden brown and crispy.

9. Cook remaining eggplant slices in the same manner and serve when ready.

Chapter8: Vegetarian

Roasted Asparagus

Servings: 4
Preparation time: 5 minutes; Active cooking time: 15 minutes; Total time: 20 minutes

Nutrition Value:
Calories: 55.4 Cal, Carbs: 3.1 g, Fat: 4.7 g, Protein: 1.4 g, Fiber: 1.5 g.

Ingredients:
- 12-ounce asparagus, trimmed
- 6 cherry tomatoes, halved
- 12 Greek olives, dry-cured
- 3 tablespoons olive oil
- 2-ounce full-fat feta cheese, crumbled

Method:
1. Set oven to 400 degrees F and let preheat.
2. In the meantime, take a baking sheet, add oil and then asparagus and roll until well coated with oil.
3. Place the baking sheet into the heated oven and cook for 12 minutes or until roasted.
4. Then remove baking sheet from oven, add tomatoes and continue baking for another 3 minutes or until tomatoes are roasted.
5. When done, sprinkle olives and cheese over asparagus and oil and stir until just mixed.
6. Serve immediately.

Cauliflower Parmesan Soup

Servings: 6

Preparation time: 5 minutes; Active cooking time: 35 minutes; Total time: 40 minutes

Nutrition Value:

Calories: 240 Cal, Carbs: 7 g, Fat: 20 g, Protein: 8 g, Fiber: 3 g.

Ingredients:

- 1 medium head of cauliflower, florets chopped
- 1/2 of medium white onion, peeled and sliced
- ½ of medium leek, sliced
- 4 tablespoons unsalted butter
- ¾ teaspoon salt
- ½ teaspoon cracked black pepper
- 2 tablespoons fresh thyme, chopped
- 4 tablespoons olive oil
- 1 cup grated parmesan cheese, full-fat
- 2 cups vegetable broth
- 3 cups water

Method:

1. Place a large pot over medium heat, add 2 tablespoons butter and cook until melt completely.
2. Then add onion, leek, and salt and cook for 3 to 5 minutes or until softened.
3. Add half of the chopped cauliflower florets, oil, vegetable broth, and water and stir until mixed.
4. Bring the mixture to simmer and cook for 15 minutes or until cauliflower is tender.
5. Stir in a ¾ portion of remaining cauliflower florets into the pot and continue simmering until tender.
6. In the meantime, place a frying pan over medium heat, add remaining butter, remaining chopped cauliflower florets and thyme and cook for 3 to 5 minutes or until butter starts to bubble, and cauliflower is nicely golden brown.

7. When cauliflower is cook, remove the pot from heat and blend with a stick blender until smooth.
8. Top soup with browned cauliflower and serves.

Tomato Mozzarella Salad

Servings: 8

Preparation time: 5 minutes; Active cooking time: 0 minute; Total time: 5 minutes

Nutrition Value:

Calories: 289 Cal, Carbs: 1 g, Fat: 25 g, Protein: 18 g, Fiber: 0.2 g.

Ingredients:

- 5 medium tomatoes
- 1 bunch of fresh basil leaves
- 1 teaspoon sea salt
- ½ teaspoon cracked black pepper
- 2 cups apple cider vinegar
- ¼ cup olive oil
- 32-ounce logs of fresh mozzarella cheese, full-fat

Method:

1. Cut tomato and cheese into ½-inch thick slices and then arrange these slices with basil in an alternating pattern in two rows in a small casserole dish.
2. Drizzle with oil and vinegar and season with salt and black pepper.
3. Serve immediately.

Dumplings

Servings: 6
Preparation time: 5 minutes; Active cooking time: 20 minutes; Total time: 25 minutes

Nutrition Value:
Calories: 452 Cal, Carbs: 14.4 g, Fat: 38.9 g, Protein: 14 g, Fiber: 4.3 g.

Ingredients:
- 3 medium zucchini, spiralized
- 3.5-ounce fresh spinach
- 1/3 cup almond flour
- 2 1/2 tablespoons coconut flour
- 1/2 teaspoon sea salt
- 1/2 teaspoon cracked black pepper
- 1/16 teaspoon ground nutmeg
- 3 tablespoons olive oil
- 2 medium eggs, pasture raised
- 8.8-ounce ricotta cheese, full-fat
- 1/2 cup grated Parmesan cheese, full-fat
- 3 cups tomato pasta sauce, unsweetened

Method:
1. Set oven to 350 degrees F and let preheat.
2. In the meantime, blanch spinach in boiling water for 30 seconds or until leaves wilt and let cool.
3. Then pat dry to remove excess moisture from spinach and chop and place in a bowl.
4. Add remaining ingredients except for zucchini and pasta sauce and stir until well mixed.
5. Shape mixture into 18 small dumpling balls, each about 2 teaspoons.
6. Take a heatproof dish, pour in tomato sauce and arrange dumpling in it.
7. Drizzle oil over dumpling and place baking dish into the oven to bake for 35 to 40 minutes or until top is nicely browned.

8. Serve dumpling with spiralized zucchini noodles.

Roasted Brussels Sprouts

Servings: 5

Preparation time: 5 minutes; Active cooking time: 10 minutes; Total time: 15 minutes

Nutrition Value:

Calories: 147.8 Cal, Carbs: 9.4 g, Fat: 11.6 g, Protein: 4.2 g, Fiber: 3.3 g.

Ingredients:

- 1-pound Brussels sprout
- 1 teaspoon minced garlic
- 1 tablespoon minced parsley
- 1/2 teaspoon salt
- 1/4 teaspoon cracked black pepper
- 3 tablespoons olive oil
- 2 teaspoons lemon juice
- 1 tablespoon lemon zest
- 1 tablespoon mustard paste
- 2 tablespoons grated parmesan cheese, full-fat

Method:

1. Trim Brussels sprout, rinse well, then cut into quarters and let rest for 5 minutes.
2. Take a steamer, fill with 1-inch water, add sprouts and let steam for 8 to 10 minutes or until tender.
3. In the meantime, place remaining ingredients except for cheese and lemon zest in a large bowl and stir until combined.
4. Add steamed sprouts and toss until well coated.
5. Top with cheese and lemon zest and serve.

Cauliflower Mash

Servings: 4

Preparation time: 5 minutes; Active cooking time: 20 minutes; Total time: 25 minutes

Nutrition Value:

Calories: 221 Cal, Carbs: 10.1 g, Fat: 20.4 g, Protein: 5.4 g, Fiber: 3.2 g.

Ingredients:
- 2 pounds cauliflower florets
- 1 teaspoon minced garlic
- 1 teaspoon salt
- ½ teaspoon cracked black pepper
- ½ teaspoon red pepper flakes
- ½ teaspoon turmeric powder
- 1 teaspoon lemon zest
- 2 tablespoons unsalted butter
- 1 teaspoon olive oil
- ¼ cup Greek yogurt

Method:
1. Fill a large pot half-full with water and bring to boil over medium-high heat.
2. Add cauliflower florets and boil for 15 minutes or until tender.
3. Then drain cauliflower florets well, return to pot and add garlic, butter, oil, and yogurt.
4. Blend the mixture using a stick blender until smooth, then add salt, black pepper, turmeric, and red pepper flakes and continue blending until fluffy.
5. Stir in lemon zest and serve immediately.

Braised Fennel with Lemon

Servings: 2

Preparation time: 10 minutes; Active cooking time: 1 hour and 40 minutes; Total time: 1 hour and 50 minutes

Nutrition Value:

Calories: 128 Cal, Carbs: 11.5 g, Fat: 9.3 g, Protein: 1.9 g, Fiber: 4.7 g.

Ingredients:

- 2 pounds fennel bulbs
- ¾ pound lemons
- 1 teaspoon minced garlic
- 1 ½ teaspoon sea salt
- ¾ teaspoon cracked black pepper
- 2 teaspoons fresh rosemary, chopped
- 1 teaspoon fresh thyme, chopped
- 6 tablespoons apple cider vinegar
- 1/4 cup olive oil

Method:

1. Set oven to 375 degrees F and let preheat.
2. In the meantime, slice fennel bulb into wedges, slice lemons into thin wedges and arrange in a large baking dish in a single layer.
3. Whisk together garlic, rosemary, thyme, vinegar, and oil until combined, pour this mixture evenly over vegetables in the baking dish, season with salt and black pepper and cover with aluminum foil.
4. Place this baking dish into the heated oven and bake for 1 hour, then uncover baking dish and continue baking for 30 to 40 minutes or until vegetables are roasted and crispy.
5. Serve straight away with baked chicken.

Roasted Broccoli

Servings: 4

Preparation time: 5 minutes; Active cooking time: 15 minutes; Total time: 20 minutes

Nutrition Value:

Calories: 143 Cal, Carbs: 7 g, Fat: 11 g, Protein: 3 g, Fiber: 4 g.

Ingredients:

- 4 cups broccoli florets
- 10 pitted black olives, sliced
- 1 teaspoon minced garlic
- ¼ teaspoon salt
- 1 teaspoon dried oregano
- ½ teaspoon lemon zest
- 1 tablespoon lemon juice
- 1 tablespoon olive oil

Method:

1. Set oven to 450 degrees F and let preheat.
2. In the meantime, place broccoli florets in a bowl, add garlic, salt, oil and toss until evenly coated.
3. Spread this mixture in a single layer on a baking sheet and place into the heated oven.
4. Bake for 12 to 15 minutes or until broccoli florets are tender and nicely golden brown.
5. While broccoli cook, stir together olives, lemon zest, and lemon juice.
6. When vegetables are done, transfer them to a serving dish, add olive mixture and stir until combined.
7. Serve straightaway.

Chapter9: Pork

Meatloaf

Servings: 9
Preparation time: 10 minutes; Active cooking time: 30 minutes; Total time: 40 minutes

Nutrition Value:
Calories: 325 Cal, Carbs: 14 g, Fat: 19 g, Protein: 21 g, Fiber: 3 g.

Ingredients:
- 1-pound ground beef, grass-fed
- 1-pound ground pork, pastured
- 1 tablespoon minced fresh parsley
- 1 cup minced white onion
- ½ cup almond flour
- 1 teaspoon salt
- 1/2 teaspoon ground black pepper
- 1/4 teaspoon hot pepper sauce
- 2 teaspoon Worcestershire sauce
- 2 tablespoons olive oil
- 2 teaspoons Dijon mustard
- 1/2 cup tomato ketchup
- 2 eggs, pasture-raised
- 1/4 water

Method:
1. Set oven to 350 degrees F and let preheat.
2. Take a 9 by 5-inch loaf pan, grease with oil and set aside until required.
3. Place all the ingredients except for ketchup in a large bowl and mix well until incorporated, don't over mix.
4. Spoon this mixture into loaf pan, smooth the top with a spatula and then spread ketchup on top.

5. Place the pan into the heated oven and bake for 30 minutes until cooked through.
6. When done, take out meatloaf from the pan and let rest for 10 minutes.
7. Then slice meatloaf and serve.

Pork Tenderloin

Servings: 6

Preparation time: 5 minutes; Active cooking time: 15 minutes; Total time: 20 minutes

Nutrition Value:

Calories: 330 Cal, Carbs: 0 g, Fat: 15 g, Protein: 47 g, Fiber: 0 g.

Ingredients:

- 1-pound pastured pork tenderloin, halved
- 1 ½ teaspoon salt
- ¾ teaspoon cracked black pepper
- 1 tablespoon olive oil

Method:

1. Place a large frying pan over medium heat, add oil and when hot, add pork tenderloin.
2. Cook for 5 to 7 minutes per side until nicely browned and cooked through.
3. When done, transfer pork tenderloin onto a cutting board, let sit for 5 minutes and then slice into 1-inch pieces.
4. Serve straightaway.

Dijon Pork Chops

Servings: 2

Preparation time: 5 minutes; Active cooking time: 10 minutes; Total time: 15 minutes

Nutrition Value:

Calories: 560 Cal, Carbs: 2 g, Fat: 49 g, Protein: 34 g, Fiber: 0 g.

Ingredients:

- 2 pork chops, pastured
- 1 teaspoon salt
- ½ teaspoon ground black pepper
- 2 tablespoons Dijon mustard paste
- 2 tablespoons applesauce, organic
- 6 tablespoons olive oil, divided

Method:

1. Place a large skillet pan over medium heat, add 4 tablespoons oil and when hot, add pork chops.
2. Cook for 3 to 5 minutes per side or until nicely browned on all sides.
3. In the meantime, whisk together remaining olive oil, applesauce, and mustard until combined.
4. When pork chops are cook, transfer them to serving plate and season with salt and black pepper.
5. Serve pork chops with prepared mustard sauce.

Pork Cutlets

Servings: 2
Preparation time: 5 minutes; Active cooking time: 10 minutes; Total time: 15 minutes

Nutrition Value:
Calories: 161 Cal, Carbs: 1 g, Fat: 5 g, Protein: 25 g, Fiber: 0 g.

Ingredients:
- 6 pork cutlets, pastured
- 1 ½ teaspoon minced garlic
- ½ teaspoon salt
- ¼ teaspoon cracked black pepper
- 1 teaspoon dried rosemary
- 2 tablespoons olive oil

Method:
1. Season pork cutlets with salt and black pepper.
2. Stir together rosemary and garlic and then sprinkle this mixture evenly on all side of pork cutlets.
3. Place a medium-sized frying pan over medium heat, add oil and when hot, pork cutlets.
4. Cook for 5 minutes per side until nicely golden brown and cooked through and serve.

Pork Carnitas

Servings: 12

Preparation time: 5 minutes; Active cooking time: 20 minutes; Total time: 25 minutes

Nutrition Value:

Calories: 464 Cal, Carbs: 3 g, Fat: 35 g, Protein: 33 g, Fiber: 1 g.

Ingredients:

- 2.5-pound pastured pork shoulder, fat trimmed
- 1 medium white onion, peeled and sliced
- 1 ½ teaspoon minced garlic
- 1 ½ teaspoon salt
- ¾ teaspoon ground black pepper
- 1 teaspoon red chili powder
- 1 teaspoon smoked paprika
- 1 teaspoon cumin powder
- 1 teaspoon dried thyme
- 1 teaspoon dried basil
- 1 teaspoon dried oregano
- 2 teaspoons and 4 tablespoons olive oil, divided
- 1 tablespoon lime juice
- 2 ½ cups chicken broth, pasture-raised
- 12 large lettuce leaves
- Lime wedges as needed
- 1/4 cup parsley, chopped

Method:

1. Set oven to 430 degrees F and let preheat.
2. In the meantime, whisk together salt, black pepper, red chili powder, paprika, cumin, thyme, basil, oregano, 2 teaspoons olive until smooth paste comes together.
3. Brush this paste all over the pork shoulder.
4. Take a deep roasting dish, place onion and garlic in the bottom of the dish, top seasoned pork shoulder on it and then pour in chicken stock.

5. Place the roasting dish into the heated oven and cook for 10 minutes.
6. Then reduce temperature to 320 degrees F and continue cooking for 5 hours, spooning cooking liquid over pork and turning over frequently.
7. When done, remove roasting pan from the oven and let pork rest for 20 minutes.
8. Then shred pork using two forms and mix into onion and garlic mixture until combined.
9. Place a large skillet pan over medium heat, add remaining olive oil and when hot, fry shredded pork in batches for 3 to 4 minutes or until crispy.
10. Spoon shredded pork on large lettuce, drizzle with lemon juice, top with parsley and serve as a wrap.

Pork Spare Ribs

Servings: 2

Preparation time: 5 minutes; Active cooking time: 3 hours; Total time: 3 hours and 5 minutes

Nutrition Value:

Calories: 26 Cal, Carbs: 1 g, Fat: 2 g, Protein: 0 g, Fiber: 0 g.

Ingredients:

- 2 racks of pork ribs, pastured
- 1 tablespoon sea salt
- 1/2 teaspoon cracked black pepper
- 1/2 teaspoon red chili powder
- 1 tablespoon coriander
- 1/2 teaspoon cumin
- 1/2 teaspoon cinnamon
- 2 tablespoons cocoa powder, unsweetened

Method:

1. Set oven to 350 degrees F and let preheat.
2. In the meantime, whisk together all the ingredients except for pork in a bowl and then rub this mixture on pork ribs until well coated.
3. Then cover ribs with aluminum foil and bake for 3 hours or until cooked through.
4. Serve straightaway.

Jamaican Jerk Pork Roast

Servings: 12
Preparation time: 5 minutes; Active cooking time: 1 hour and 10 minutes; Total time: 1 hour and 15 minutes

Nutrition Value:
Calories: 296 Cal, Carbs: 6 g, Fat: 20 g, Protein: 23 g, Fiber: 0 g.

Ingredients:
- 4 pounds pastured pork shoulder, fat trimmed
- 1/4 cup Jamaican Jerk spice blend
- 1 tablespoon olive oil
- 1/2 cup beef broth, grass-fed

Method:
1. Brush roast with olive oil and then season well with the spice blend.
2. Plug in instant pot, press the sauté button, add oil to the inner pot and when hot, add pork.
3. Cook for 5 to 7 minutes per side or until brown on all side and then pour in beef broth.
4. Press the cancel button, shut instant pot with its lid, press manual button and cook for 45 minutes at high pressure.
5. When instant pot beeps, press the cancel button and do quick pressure release.
6. Open the lid, take out pork shoulder, shred and serve.

Pulled Pork

Servings: 8

Preparation time: 5 minutes; Active cooking time: 4 hours; Total time: 4 hours and 5 minutes

Nutrition Value:

Calories: 236 Cal, Carbs: 2 g, Fat: 11 g, Protein: 30 g, Fiber: 2 g.

Ingredients:

- 3 pounds boneless pastured pork shoulder, fat trimmed
- 2 teaspoons onion powder
- 2 teaspoons garlic powder
- 2 teaspoons salt
- 2 teaspoons paprika
- 1 tablespoon dried parsley
- 1 teaspoon dried rosemary
- 1 teaspoon dried thyme
- 2 teaspoons cumin
- ½ cup beer

Method:

1. Stir together all the ingredients except for pork until combined and then rub this mixture all over pork shoulder.
2. Place this pork shoulder to a 6-quart slow cooker, pour in beer and then shut with its lid.
3. Plug in the slow cooker and cook pork for 4 hours at high heat setting until pork is very tender.
4. When done, shred pork with two forks, stir well into cooking liquid and serve.

Chapter 10: Beef

Sun-Dried Tomato Cheesy Meatballs

Servings: 2
Preparation time: 0 minutes; Active cooking time: 30 minutes; Total time: 40 minutes

Nutrition Value:
Calories: 496 Cal, Carbs: 13.6 g, Fat: 27.8 g, Protein: 44.8 g, Fiber: 1 g.

Ingredients:
FOR THE MEATBALLS:
- 18-ounce ground beef, grass-fed
- 18-ounce ground pork, pasture-raised
- 6-ounce sun-dried tomatoes, drained
- 2 teaspoons minced garlic
- 1 tablespoon salt
- ½ tablespoon ground black pepper
- 1 tablespoon fresh chopped oregano
- 1 tablespoon fresh chopped basil
- 1/2 cup almond flour
- 1 tablespoon olive oil and more for greasing
- 4 tablespoons tomato paste
- 1 egg, pasture-raised
- 1/2 cup grated parmesan cheese, full-fat

FOR THE SAUCE:
- 28-ounce tomato pasta sauce
- 6 large Bocconcini balls, sliced
- ½ cup sun-dried tomato oil

Method:
1. Place all the ingredients for meatballs in a large bowl, stir until well mixed and then shape mixture into 12 meatballs.

2. Place a large skillet pan over medium heat, grease with oil and when hot, add meatballs in a single layer.
3. Cook for 3 to 4 minutes per side until nicely browned on all sides and cooked through.
4. When done, transfer meatballs to a plate and cook remaining meatballs in the same manner.
5. Into the pan, add sun-dried oil and when hot, add tomato sauce.
6. Cook for 2 minutes, then return meatballs to pan and bring to boil.
7. Then reduce heat to a low level and simmer meatballs for 15 to 20 minutes or until meatballs are cook through and sauce is thickened.
8. Meanwhile, switch on a broiler over medium heat.
9. When meatballs are cooked through, remove the pan from heat, add cheese balls and place the pan under the broiler.
10. Broil meatballs for 3 to 5 minutes or until cheese melts and then serve.

Rib-eye Steak with Gremolata

Servings: 2
Preparation time: 5 minutes; Active cooking time: 20 minutes; Total time: 25 minutes

Nutrition Value:
Calories: 722 Cal, Carbs: 1.8 g, Fat: 62.2 g, Protein: 38.1 g, Fiber: 0.5 g.

Ingredients:
For Steaks:

- 2 small rib-eye steaks, grass-fed
- 1/4 teaspoon salt
- 1/4 teaspoon ground black pepper
- 1 tablespoon olive oil and more for cooking

For Gremolata

- 4 tablespoons freshly chopped parsley
- 1 teaspoon minced garlic
- 2 teaspoon lemon zest
- 3 tablespoons olive oil

Method:

1. Brush steaks with oil, then season with salt and black pepper.
2. Place a large frying pan over high heat, add oil and when hot, add seasoned steaks.
3. Cook for 3 to 4 minutes until meat is no longer pink and browned, then flip the steak and continue cooking for another 4 minutes.
4. Then reduce heat to medium level and continue cooking for 4 to 11 minutes or until steak is cook to the desired level.
5. When done, transfer the steaks to a plate and let rest for 5 to 7 minutes.
6. In the meantime, stir together all the ingredients for Gremolata.
7. Serve steaks with Gremolata.

Beef Stir-Fry

Servings: 4
Preparation time: 5 minutes; Active cooking time: 15 minutes; Total time: 20 minutes

Nutrition Value:
Calories: 416 Cal, Carbs: 20 g, Fat: 27 g, Protein: 25 g, Fiber: 7 g.

Ingredients:
- 1-pound ground beef, cut into bite-size pieces
- 2 red bell peppers, diced
- 1/4 cup cilantro, chopped
- 3 medium tomatoes, diced
- 1/2 of medium white onion, peeled and diced
- 1 teaspoon minced garlic
- 1 teaspoon salt
- ½ teaspoon ground black pepper
- 1 teaspoon hot sauce
- 2 tablespoons olive oil

Method:
1. Place a medium skillet pan over medium-high heat, add oil and when hot, add beef.
2. Cook for 5 to 8 minutes or until beef is nicely browned and then transfer beef to a plate.
3. Add pepper, tomato, and onion to the pan and cook for 5 minutes.
4. Return ground beef to pan and continue cooking until beef is cook through and vegetables are tender.
5. Then add remaining ingredients, stir well and cook for 2 minutes.
6. Serve when ready.

Sesame Beef

Servings: 4

Preparation time: 10 minutes; Active cooking time: 15 minutes; Total time: 25 minutes

Nutrition Value:
Calories: 412.3 Cal, Carbs: 8.8 g, Fat: 31.3 g, Protein: 24.5 g, Fiber: 3.8 g.

Ingredients:
- 1-pound, grass-fed sirloin steak, sliced into thin strips
- 4 tablespoons almond flour, divided
- 1 cup peanut oil

For the Sauce:
- 1 green onion, thinly sliced
- 1 teaspoon minced garlic
- 1 tablespoon grated ginger
- 1/4 cup brown sugar
- 1/4 cup soy sauce
- 2 tablespoons apple cider vinegar
- 1 tablespoon Sriracha sauce
- 2 tablespoons orange juice
- 1 teaspoon sesame oil
- 1 teaspoon sesame seeds

Method:
1. Place steak strips to a large bowl, add 2 tablespoons almond flour and toss until coat.
2. Then sprinkle with remaining 2 tablespoons cornstarch.
3. Place a large skillet pan over medium heat, add peanut oil and when hot, add steak strips in a single layer and cook for 3 minutes until crispy.
4. Cook remaining steak strips in the same manner and then transfer to a plate lined with paper towel.
5. Whisk together garlic, ginger, sugar, soy sauce, vinegar, Sriracha sauce, orange juice, sesame oil and add to a medium saucepan.

6. Place this saucepan over medium-high heat and cook for 2 minutes or until slightly thick.
7. Add steak and stir until combined.
8. Garnish with sesame seeds and green onion and serve.

Mediterranean Burgers

Servings: 4
Preparation time: 10 minutes; Active cooking time: 12 minutes; Total time: 22 minutes

Nutrition Value:
Calories: 443 Cal, Carbs: 4 g, Fat: 34 g, Protein: 25 g, Fiber: 0.6 g.

Ingredients:
- 1 1/2 pounds ground beef, grass-fed
- 1 teaspoon salt
- 3/4 teaspoon ground black pepper, divided
- 2 teaspoons minced fresh oregano
- 2 teaspoons fresh rosemary
- 1 tablespoon grated lemon zest
- 6 ounces crumbled feta cheese, full-fat
- 2 tablespoons olive oil
- 4 large lettuce leaves for serving

Method:
1. Place all the ingredients except for oil in a large bowl and stir until well combined.
2. Then shape mixture into four patties.
3. Preheat a grill over medium heat, then grease with grilling grate with oil and place patties on it.
4. Grill for 5 to 6 minutes per side until nicely browned and cooked through.
5. Serve patties as a lettuce wrap.

Sirloin Beef Roast

Servings: 6

Preparation time: 10 minutes; Active cooking time: 1 hour and 30 minutes; Total time: 1 hour and 40 minutes

Nutrition Value:

Calories: 248 Cal, Carbs: 1.5 g, Fat: 5.7 g, Protein: 44.2 g, Fiber: 0.3 g.

Ingredients:

- 2-pound beef roast, grass-fed
- 2 medium zucchini, cut into 1-inch chunks
- 2 medium butternut squash, cut into 1-inch chunks
- 1/2 cup cherry tomato, halved
- 1 teaspoon salt, divided
- 1/8 teaspoon cracked black pepper
- 1 teaspoon dried basil, divided
- 1/2 teaspoon dried oregano
- 1 tablespoon lemon juice
- 3 tablespoons olive oil, divided

Method:

1. Set oven to 325 degrees F and let preheat.
2. Whisk together ½ teaspoon salt, black pepper, ½ teaspoon basil, oregano, and 1 tablespoon oil until well mixed and then rub this mixture all over beef roast.
3. Place the beef in a roasting pan and bake for 45 minutes.
4. Meanwhile, whisk together remaining salt and basil, lemon juice and remaining olive oil in a large bowl.
5. Add zucchini, squash, and tomato and toss until well coated.
6. After 45 minutes of roasting, place seasoned vegetables around the beef and continue roasting for another 45 minutes until beef is medium done.
7. When done, slice roast and serve with vegetables.

Beef & Broccoli

Servings: 4

Preparation time: 5 minutes; Active cooking time: 3 hours and 30 minutes; Total time: 3 hours and 35 minutes

Nutrition Value:

Calories: 329 Cal, Carbs: 11 g, Fat: 19 g, Protein: 26 g, Fiber: 2 g.

Ingredients:

- 1-pound grass-fed steak, sliced
- 12 ounces broccoli florets, fresh
- 2 teaspoons minced garlic
- 1/8 teaspoon grated ginger
- 1/4 teaspoon red pepper flakes
- 1/2 teaspoon liquid monk fruit
- 1/2 teaspoon xanthan gum
- 1/3 cup tamari
- 1 tablespoon olive oil
- 1 cup beef broth

Method:

1. Place steak in a 6-quart slow cooker, add remaining ingredients except for xanthan gum and stir until mixed.
2. Plug in the slow cooker, shut with its lid and cook for 3 hours at low heat setting until cooked through.
3. Then stir in xanthan gum and stir until well mixed.
4. Continue slow cooking for 30 minutes at low heat setting and serve when ready.

Eggplant Ground Beef Skillet

Servings: 6
Preparation time: 5 minutes; Active cooking time: 23 minutes; Total time: 28 minutes

Nutrition Value:
Calories: 209 Cal, Carbs: 6.3 g, Fat: 13.8 g, Protein: 15.7 g, Fiber: 4.2 g.

Ingredients:
- 1-pound ground beef, grass-fed
- 1 medium eggplant, diced
- 2 cups tomato, chopped
- 1 teaspoon minced garlic
- 1/4 teaspoon salt
- 1 tablespoon soy sauce
- 1 tablespoon olive oil

Method:
1. Place a large skillet pan over medium heat, add olive oil and when hot, add eggplant and season with salt.
2. Cook for 3 to 5 minutes or until soften and then transfer to a bowl.
3. Into the pan, add ground beef and garlic and cook for 7 to 10 minutes or until meat is nicely browned.
4. Return eggplant to pan, add tomato and soy sauce and cook for 2 to 3 minutes or until liquid is evaporated.
5. Serve straightaway.

Chapter11: Seafood & Fish

Swordfish

Servings: 4
Preparation time: 1 hour and 10 minutes; Active cooking time: 12 minutes; Total time: 1 hour and 22 minutes

Nutrition Value:
Calories: 226.9 Cal, Carbs: 1 g, Fat: 11.3 g, Protein: 23 g, Fiber: 0.1 g.

Ingredients:
- 4 wild-caught swordfish steaks, each about 7 ounces
- 12 cloves of garlic, peeled
- 3/4 teaspoon salt
- 1/2 teaspoon ground black pepper
- 1 teaspoon paprika
- 1 teaspoon coriander
- 1 1/2 teaspoon ground cumin
- 3 tablespoons lemon juice
- 1/3 cup olive oil

Method:
1. Place all the ingredients except for swordfish in a blender and pulse until smooth.
2. Pat dry swordfish steaks, then apply spice rub generously on all sides, then cover with aluminum foil and let marinate for 1 hour in the refrigerator.
3. When ready to cook, preheat a griddle pan over high heat, grease with oil and when hot, add swordfish steaks.
4. Cook for 5 to 6 minutes per side until nicely browned and cooked through.
5. Serve straightaway.

Garlic Shrimp Zoodles

Servings: 2

Preparation time: 5 minutes; Active cooking time: 5 minutes; Total time: 10 minutes

Nutrition Value:

Calories: 308.4 Cal, Carbs: 10.3 g, Fat: 14.8 g, Protein: 33.5 g, Fiber: 3.2 g.

Ingredients:

- 2 medium zucchini, spiralized
- 3/4 pounds wild-caught medium shrimp, peeled & deveined
- 2 tablespoons chopped fresh parsley
- 2 teaspoons minced garlic
- 1 teaspoon salt
- ½ teaspoon cracked black pepper
- 1 tablespoon olive oil
- 1 lemon, juiced and zested

Method:

1. Place a medium skillet pan over medium heat, add oil, lemon juice, and zest and when hot, add shrimps.
2. Cook shrimps for 1 minute per side, then season with garlic and red pepper flakes and continue cooking for 1 minute.
3. Then add zucchini noodles, toss until well mixed and cook for 3 minutes or until warm through.
4. Season with salt and black pepper, garnish with parsley and serve straightaway.

Salmon with Asparagus

Servings: 2
Preparation time: 5 minutes; Active cooking time: 15 minutes; Total time: 20 minutes

Nutrition Value:
Calories: 632 Cal, Carbs: 6 g, Fat: 54.7 g, Protein: 30.6 g, Fiber: 2.7 g.

Ingredients:
- 2 small wild-caught salmon fillets
- 8.8-ounce bunch asparagus
- 1 ½ teaspoon salt, divided
- 1 teaspoon ground black pepper, divided
- 1 tablespoon olive oil
- 1 cup hollandaise sauce, low-carb

Method:
1. Season salmon fillets with 1 teaspoon salt and ½ teaspoon ground black pepper
2. Place a large skillet pan over medium heat, add oil and when hot, add seasoned salmon fillets and cook for 4 to 5 minutes per side until seared.
3. Move salmon fillet to a side of the pan, add asparagus to other side of pan and season with remaining salt and black pepper and cook for 5 minutes.
4. Serve salmon with asparagus and hollandaise sauce.

Tuna Salad

Servings: 4

Preparation time: 5 minutes; Active cooking time: 0 minute; Total time: 5 minutes

Nutrition Value:

Calories: 651 Cal, Carbs: 8.7 g, Fat: 54.6 g, Protein: 32.6 g, Fiber: 3.9 g.

Ingredients:

- 10-ounce cooked tuna, wild-caught
- 1/4 cup chopped kalamata olives
- 2 large tomatoes
- 2 tablespoons chopped fire-roasted red peppers
- 2 tablespoons minced red onion
- 2 tablespoons chopped fresh basil
- ¾ teaspoon salt
- ½ teaspoon cracked black pepper
- 1 tablespoon lemon juice
- 1/4 cup mayonnaise, full-fat
- 1 tablespoon capers

Method:

1. Place all the ingredients in a salad bowl, except for tomatoes and stir until combined.
2. Open each tomato by slice into the sixth, without cutting all the way through, and then scoop salad into the center.
3. Serve straightaway.

Seared Scallops

Servings: 4

Preparation time: 5 minutes; Active cooking time: 10 minutes; Total time: 15 minutes

Nutrition Value:

Calories: 289 Cal, Carbs: 5.7 g, Fat: 22.7 g, Protein: 15.9 g, Fiber: 0.4 g.

Ingredients:

- 1.1-pound fresh scallops, trimmed
- 4 tablespoons fresh chopped parsley
- 1 tablespoon fresh chopped chives
- ½ teaspoon minced garlic
- ¾ teaspoon salt
- ½ teaspoon cracked black pepper
- 1 lemon, juiced and zested
- 3 tablespoons olive oil
- 4 tablespoons unsalted butter
- 1/3 cup chicken broth, pasture-raised

Method:

1. Place a large frying pan over high heat, add oil and when hot, add scallops in a single layer and cook for 3 minutes.
2. Cook remaining scallops in the same manner and transfer to a plate.
3. Into the pan, add 3 tablespoons butter and garlic and cook for 2 minutes or until nicely golden brown.
4. Add lemon juice and zest, remaining butter, stir until well mixed and then return scallops to the pan.
5. Cook for 3 minutes or until warm through and serve straightaway.

Grilled Sardines

Servings: 4

Preparation time: 5 minutes; Active cooking time: 20 minutes; Total time: 25 minutes

Nutrition Value:

Calories: 411 Cal, Carbs: 3 g, Fat: 33.7 g, Protein: 32.5 g, Fiber: 1.1 g.

Ingredients:

- 8 large wild-caught sardines, scaled and cleaned
- 1 teaspoon salt
- ¾ teaspoon ground black pepper
- 1 tablespoon chopped thyme
- 1 tablespoon chopped rosemary
- 1 tablespoon chopped basil leaves
- 1 lemon, halved
- 1/4 cup olive oil
- ½ cup tomato salsa, fresh

Method:

1. Brush sardine with oil and then season well with salt, black pepper, thyme, rosemary, and basil.
2. Place the griddle pan, grease with oil and when hot, add seasoned sardines in a single layer along with lemon halved and let cook for 3 minutes per side until cooked through and charred.
3. Cook remaining sardines in the same manner and serve with charred lemon and tomato salsa.

Salmon Cakes

Servings: 8
Preparation time: 10 minutes; Active cooking time: 30 minutes; Total time: 40 minutes

Nutrition Value:
Calories: 155 Cal, Carbs: 3 g, Fat: 7 g, Protein: 20 g, Fiber: 1.2 g.

Ingredients:
- 1½ cups cooked salmon, wild-caught
- 1 stalk of celery, diced
- 1 small white onion, peeled and chopped
- ½ teaspoon cracked black pepper
- 3 tablespoons chopped fresh dill
- 1½ cups almond flour
- 2 teaspoons Dijon mustard
- 3 teaspoons olive oil, divided
- 1 pasture-raised egg, lightly beaten

Method:
1. Set oven to 425 degrees F and let preheat.
2. In the meantime, place a large skillet pan over medium-high heat, add 1 ½ teaspoons oil and when hot, add onion and celery.
3. Cook for 3 minutes or until softened, then stir in dill and remove the pan from heat.
4. Place salmon in a bowl, break into small piece with a fork, then add cooked onion mixture, black pepper, and almond flour and mix well until combined.
5. Shape this mixture into 8 patties.
6. Return skillet pan to medium heat, add remaining oil and when hot, add patties in a single layer and cook for 3 minutes per side.
7. Cook remaining patties in the same manner and transfer to a baking sheet, lined with aluminum foil and greased with oil.
8. Place this baking sheet into the oven and bake for 15 minutes or until nicely golden brown and cooked through.

9. In the meantime, prepare yogurt dill sauce and for this, stir together all the ingredients for the sauce until combined.
10. Serve salmon cakes with prepared yogurt dill sauce.

Mussels

Servings: 6
Preparation time: 5 minutes; Active cooking time: 15 minutes; Total time: 20 minutes

Nutrition Value:
Calories: 237 Cal, Carbs: 7.1 g, Fat: 13 g, Protein: 23 g, Fiber: 2.6 g.

Ingredients:
- 2 pounds wild-caught mussels, shelled
- ½ cup chopped parsley
- 1 medium white onion, peeled and chopped
- 1 teaspoon minced garlic
- 1/2 teaspoon salt
- 1/8 teaspoon cayenne pepper
- 2 tablespoons olive oil
- 1 tablespoon tomato paste
- 2-ounce crumbled feta cheese, full-fat
- 1 cup white wine

Method:
1. Set oven to 390 degrees F and let preheat.
2. Place a medium skillet pan over medium heat, add oil and when hot, add onion and cook for 3 minutes or until tender.
3. Add mussels, tomato, salt and wine, stir, bring the mixture to boil and continue boiling until wine evaporates completely.
4. Then stir in garlic and cayenne pepper and simmer for 5 minutes, set aside until required.
5. Place mussels in a bowl, add cheese and parsley and place on a baking dish.
6. Bake mussels for 5 to 7 minutes or until cheese melts completely and mussels are nicely golden brown.
7. Serve mussels with prepared tomato sauce.

Chapter 12: Desserts

Crème Anglaise

Servings: 2
Preparation time: 5 minutes; Active cooking time: 10 minutes; Total time: 15 minutes

Nutrition Value:
Calories: 294 Cal, Carbs: 2.7 g, Fat: 29.3 g, Protein: 3.2 g, Fiber: 0 g.

Ingredients:
- 6 tablespoons Erythritol
- 1 teaspoon vanilla extract, unsweetened
- 5 egg yolks, pasture-raised
- 2 cups coconut milk, unsweetened and full-fat

Method:
1. Place a medium saucepan over medium heat, add vanilla and coconut milk and whisk until combined and bring to simmer.
2. In the meantime, whisk together egg yolks and Erythritol until blended.
3. Slowly whisk in milk mixture, then return this mixture to pan over medium heat and cook for 3 to 5 minutes or until thickened to the desired level.
4. When done, let the custard cool slightly and then serve with sliced fruits.

Chocolate Mousse

Servings: 4
Preparation time: 2 hours and 5 minutes; Active cooking time: 5 minutes; Total time: 2 hours and 10 minutes

Nutrition Value:
Calories: 346 Cal, Carbs: 6 g, Fat: 30 g, Protein: 3.5 g, Fiber: 2.5 g.

Ingredients:
- 3.5-ounce dark chocolate, chopped
- 1 tablespoon Erythritol
- 1/2 teaspoon vanilla extract, unsweetened
- 2 cups Greek yogurt
- 3/4 cup almond milk, unsweetened and full-fat

Method:
1. Place a medium saucepan over medium heat, add chocolate and simmer for 3 to 5 minutes or until chocolate melts completely, whisking frequently.
2. Then whisk in vanilla and sweetener until dissolved and then remove the pan from heat.
3. Place yogurt in a large bowl, pour in chocolate mixture and mix until well combined.
4. Divide this mixture evenly between 4 serving bowls and let chill in the refrigerator for 2 hours.
5. When done, top with raspberries and serve.

Mint Chocolate Chip Ice Cream

Servings: 1
Preparation time: 3 hours; Active cooking time: 0 minutes; Total time: 3 hours

Nutrition Value:
Calories: 151 Cal, Carbs: 3.5 g, Fat: 15 g, Protein: 1.5 g, Fiber: 2 g.

Ingredients:
- 2 tablespoons chocolate chips, unsweetened
- 1 teaspoon cocoa powder, unsweetened
- 1/16 teaspoon salt
- 1/16 teaspoon Erythritol
- 1/4 teaspoon vanilla extract, unsweetened
- 6 drops peppermint extract, unsweetened
- 1 cup coconut milk, unsweetened and full-fat

Method:
1. Place all the ingredients in a large bowl and whisk using a stand mixer until well combined.
2. Pour this mixture in a freezer proof container, seal the container and place in freezer for 2 to 3 hours until frozen.
3. Then remove bowl from the freezer, let rest at room temperature for 15 minutes or until slightly softened and then blend again with a stand mixer.
4. Serve straightaway.

Chocolate Avocado Pudding

Servings: 2
Preparation time: 5 minutes; Active cooking time: 20 minutes; Total time: 25 minutes

Nutrition Value:
Calories: 331 Cal, Carbs: 15 g, Fat: 32 g, Protein: 5 g, Fiber: 10 g.

Ingredients:
- 1 medium avocado, pitted
- 1/4 cup cocoa powder, unsweetened
- 1 teaspoon sea salt
- 1/2 teaspoon vanilla extract, unsweetened
- 10 drops liquid stevia

Method:
1. Remove it from avocado, then scoop out its flesh and place in a bowl.
2. Add remaining ingredients and blend using a stick blender until well combined.
3. Serve immediately.

Vanilla Frozen Yogurt

Servings: 8
Preparation time: 35 minutes; Active cooking time: 0 minute; Total time: 35 minutes

Nutrition Value:
Calories: 122 Cal, Carbs: 2.7 g, Fat: 11.4 g, Protein: 3.2 g, Fiber: 0 g.

Ingredients:
- 4 tablespoons monk fruit sweetener, grounded
- 2 teaspoons vanilla extract, unsweetened
- 1 tablespoon lemon juice
- 1 tablespoon olive oil
- 3 cups chilled plain yogurt, full fat

Method:
1. Place all the ingredients in a blender and pulse for 1 to 2 minutes or until blended and creamy.
2. Spoon this mixture into a freezer safe container, cover with its lid and chill for 30 minutes or until soft but firm ice cream comes together.
3. Serve straightaway.

Chia Berry Yogurt Parfaits

Servings: 4
Preparation time: 10 minutes; Active cooking time: 0 minutes; Total time: 10 minutes

Nutrition Value:
Calories: 319 Cal, Carbs: 15.3 g, Fat: 25.1 g, Protein: 12.1 g, Fiber: 7.6 g.

Ingredients:
- 1 cup mixed berries, frozen
- 1/3 cup flaked coconut, toasted
- 1/3 cup chia seeds
- 2 tablespoons sunflower seeds
- 2 tablespoons pumpkin seeds
- 1 tablespoon Erythritol
- 1/4 teaspoon ground cinnamon
- 1/2 teaspoon vanilla extract, unsweetened
- 1/2 cup coconut cream, full-fat
- 1 cup Greek yogurt
- 2/3 cup water

Method:
1. Stir together chia seeds, Erythritol, cinnamon, vanilla, coconut cream, and water until well combined and then spoon in a bottom of a serving bowl.
2. Mix berries and yogurt with a fork until crushed and smooth paste form and then spoon this mixture in an even layer on top of the chia seed layer.
3. Stir together sunflower seeds, pumpkin seeds and coconut flakes and top this mixture on the berries-yogurt layer.
4. Serve straightaway.

Lemon Meringue Cookies

Servings: 15
Preparation time: 2 hours and 10 minutes; Active cooking time: 1 hour; Total time: 3 hours and 10 minutes

Nutrition Value:
Calories: 2 Cal, Carbs: 0 g, Fat: 0 g, Protein: 0.5 g, Fiber: 0 g.

Ingredients:
- 1/4 cup Erythritol
- 1/2 tablespoon lemon zest
- 1/2 teaspoon lemon juice
- 2 egg whites, pasture-raised

Method:
1. Set oven to 200 degrees F and let preheat.
2. In the meantime, place egg whites in a large bowl and blend using a stick blender until stiff peaks forms.
3. Then beat in lemon juice until hard peaks forms and then beat in sweetener, 1 tablespoon at a time, until well mixed and slowly beat in lemon zest.
4. Spoon this mixture into a piping bag and form cookies on a baking sheet, lined with a parchment sheet.
5. Place the baking sheet into the heated oven and bake for 1 hour, then switch off the oven and let cookies rest in oven for 1 to 2 hours until cool completely.
6. Serve straightaway.

Strawberry Cheesecake Jars

Servings: 4

Preparation time: 1 hour and 10 minutes; Active cooking time: 0 minutes; Total time: 1 hour and 10 minutes

Nutrition Value:
Calories: 375 Cal, Carbs: 6.9 g, Fat: 36.5 g, Protein: 4.3 g, Fiber: 1.2 g.

Ingredients:
- 1 cup and 1 tablespoon strawberry and basil chia jam
- 1/4 cup powdered Erythritol
- 1 teaspoon lemon zest
- 1/2 teaspoon vanilla extract, unsweetened
- 1 tablespoon lemon juice
- 1 cup coconut cream, full-fat
- 1 cup cream cheese, full-fat
- 1/2 cup sour cream, full-fat

Method:
1. Beat together lemon zest, vanilla, coconut cream, and cream cheese with a stick blender until smooth.
2. Divide this mixture evenly into 6 jars, each about 4-ounce, then top with 2 tablespoons of strawberry and basil chia jam.
3. Place these jars in the refrigerator for 1 hour or until chilled and then serve.

Conclusion

Indeed, high-fat Ketogenic diet is the quickest way to smartness and attaining a fit body. The Ketogenic diet is evident for its amazing health benefits, especially physical fitness. Then, what about mental wellness?

Following a diet shouldn't always be consuming healthy foods that is high in fats. One should also have a healthy lifestyle like adopting quality habits that create positive impacts on mind, heart, and soul. You can achieve the best of these both worlds by following Ketogenic diet influenced with the Mediterranean diet.

The Ketogenic Mediterranean is much more than having healthy eating habits. When implemented in the right manner with true devotion, it can completely change your life for the better.

Made in the USA
Middletown, DE
18 June 2019